Insights and Outlooks

By Linda Stitt

    Reflections from a dusty mirror
    What do you feed a unicorn?
    Yesterday's poetry
    It was true at the time

Insights and Outlooks

Linda Stitt

Sadhana Press

Toronto

© 1991 Sadhana Press
c/o 44 St. Joseph Street, #2112
Toronto, Ontario, Canada
M4Y 2W4

Distributed by
Natural Heritage/Natural History Inc.
P.O. Box 69, Station H
Toronto, Ontario
M4C 5H7

All rights reserved. No portion of this book may be reproduced in any form or by any means whatsoever without written permission, except in the case of brief quotations embodied in critical articles and reviews.

Cover design by Molly Brass
Front cover photo by David Fleishman
Author photograph by Samuel Ginsburg

Set in 12 point Adobe Garamond

Canadian Cataloguing in Publication Data

Stitt, Linda, 1932–
 Insights and outlooks

Poems.
ISBN 0-9691296-4-5

I. Title

PS8587.T5715 1991   C811'.54   C91-094944-1
PR9199.3.S7515 1991

Printed in Canada on recycled paper

This book is for
my mother,
who gives me
meaning,
purpose,
inspiration
and unconditional love.

It is offered, with gratitude, to those friends who have requested it and to those friends whose assistance has made it possible.

Special thanks to Don Brill for his procedural perspicacity, to Morley Chalmers for his talented typesetting, to David Fleishman for his consummate cover photography, to Marie Hopps, George Ghent and Charlene Jones for their editing expertise, and to Barry Penhale for his faith, hope and charity.

Contents

Outlook 1
Telepathy/telegony – tropology 2
Adios comparison 4
Objective observation 5
Ad nauseam 6
To be specific 7
Summit as pique experience (Toronto – 1988) 8
Show stopper in the human circus 9
On the shady side of the street 10
Last gasp 11
The buck stops there 12
Out of my hands 13
Simple request 14
Old gods 15
Personal opinion on an old philosophical question 16
A lesson from Mum 17
The First Noble Truth 18
Earth Day – 1990 19
The sophisticates 20
Safe for the moment 21
Healing 22
Purification 23
People 24
Omigods 25
May 26
I do knot 27
Things are sometimes what they seem 28
New Year's Resolution II 29
White Boots poem 30
Single minded and selfish to the end 32
Limitations 33
Mantra 34
Runaway 35
As my father lay dying 36

Weeded out	37
Foretaste	38
Lioness' share	39
Showtime	40
April	41
No–body witness	42
Star dust	43
Jane makes hospital calls	44
Ten seconds to midnight – a round	45
Reconciliation	46
Laboratory rabbits	47
The survivor	48
No trouble at all	49
Design fault	50
Toronto – Victoria Day	51
Fowl fornication	52
Keeping on	54
New Year's Day – 1990	55
Love thy neighbour	56
Sic transit	57
The pessimist	58
Thank you not	59
Who?	60
Mother of the bride	61
Cycling	62
Unhappy hour	63
Sound mind – unsound body	64
Short leash	65
Reality therapy	66
Overextended	67
Post-mortem	68
Elaboration	69
Deux ex tenuated	70
City mouse	71
Starlings	72
New ground	73

Hope springs	74
Youth passing	75
Croaked	76
Farewell	77
Always the longing	78
Busy, busy	79
Reminiscences	80
Prolonged adolescence	81
A loner with a lover	82
In my prime	84
The intuitive rose	85
Seas apart	86
Another love poem – for my old friends	87
Rapunzel in the city	88
A gift of ammonite…	89
I wish	90
Seasoning	91
Passing through	92
Wake-up call	93
Taxidermy (stuff this)	94
The great, collective shame	95
For Ruth	96
Observation by an almost complete donkey	97
Epitaph	98
Nothing doing	99
Extinction	100
November sixteenth	101
Highest authority	102
Global concern	103
Silk purse	104
Discretion	105
In my dreams	106
Intermittent affair	108
Minor move	109
Capital litter	110
Shame on me	111

Disorient express	112
…to the world	113
Travel fare	114
Requiem	115
Imperfect love	116
Cosmos	117
Broken silence	118
The sycophants	119
Better late	120
Immediate family	121
Awedball	122
Poet emeritus	123
Pollution control	124
Disciple	125
Koan in circles	126
Another lesson from Mum	127
Out of play	128
Concrastination	129
Still gestating	130
Moment um	131
Rat race	132
Dealer's choice	133
Not even edgewise	134
Diligence	135
Directions	136
Publix spectacle	137
Relocation	138
The builder	139
Sometime	140
Gesture	141
Insight	142

Insights and Outlooks

Outlook

Well, I'm fairly sure the universe
is doing what is best
for my interests, and it may be that
the whole thing is a test
and, although I have conceded
it is surely for the good,
it just looks like one more lesson
that I haven't understood.

Telepathy/telegony – tropology

      All my loves
and all my lovers
have favoured me
with some ejaculate,
some seminal thought
transported in the pullulating fluid
drawn from the aggregate ocean,
and every intercourse
has impregnated me
with ideas
offsprung
as much from sperm as egg.
      So I have borne
no parthenogenic poetry,
nor is the womb of inspiration
cleansed with every issue
but carries still
the essence of a thousand seedings.
      Consequently,
I conceive
no purebred progeny,
only mongrel spawn
of multiple interminglings
of consciousness.

Then if,
within my swaddling thoughts
you recognize
some feature of yourself,
some mirrored musing,
some reflected notion,
it may occur to you
that,
gender notwithstanding
and meeting long since past,
or never joined,
you have been,
through some old incorporeal coupling,
begetter
to my anomalous child.

Adios comparison

Some poets are scholars or prophets
or sages, who fill up their pages
with weighty, profound revelations
and write for the ages.
But I am more simple, less solemn,
just someone who natters and chatters
and writes for the sisters and brothers
of family matters.

Objective observation

I am mildly amused, faintly frightened
by the theoretically enlightened
whose knowledge hasn't opened their eyes –
just taught them how to rationalize.

Ad nauseam

Our planet grows sickly and pale
as gentlemen, robust and ruddy,
commission a study
and,
on its completion,
a study
········to study
················the study.

To be specific

Although specifics
might be wise,
I generally
generalize,
missing the star
for the constellation,
the individual
for the nation,
losing the heifer
in the herd,
seeing the flock
and not the bird.
I shall take it
as a goal
to see the parts
within the whole.
All species speak
of interlinked
units, special
and distinct.
Each galaxy
has many suns
and every group
is made of ones
and, in the forest,
so to speak,
every tree
should stand unique.
Diversity observed
engenders
reverence
for creation's
splendours.

Summit as pique experience
(Toronto – 1988)

To this city where I dwell
has come the foetid, martial scent
of uniform and armament
and folk who do not love me well.
The pavement is no longer mine;
I have no access to my street
where those I do not care to meet
are guarded as they go to dine
in the establishment of greed
and power. And while those who lead
the followers will safely feed,
I disavow the want or need
for lethal germs of violence
which by their black example, breed.
The mighty in their motorcades,
the righteous in their limousines
are treated to cosmetic scenes,
the most expensive ever made.
Those citizens who find a fault
as skies are curdled, nights are churned,
will be efficiently interned,
denouncing such benign assault.
And the innocent bear the burden of proof
and the price of prestige, and few protest
for surely our leaders know what's best.
So sleep sound, baby, there's a cop on the roof.

Show stopper in the human circus

I watch with grief and disbelief
the death-defying stunt of us
scorching our earth – left, right, behind,
and burning our bridges in front of us.

On the shady side of the street

The bridge to serenity seems uncrossable;
tranquillity appears impossible;
equanimity is a mockery.
Let us go and hurl some crockery.

Last gasp

The world is sick with war and waste,
with ignorance and greed.
Good will, good sense would see we have
as much as we could need.

We squabble and we squander,
we ravage and we fight
like savage wart hogs,
sadly short of temper and of sight.

We kill for sport and pleasure
and love ourselves no less.
We sell our children's future
to buy today's excess.

We talk of moderation
and talk and talk and talk
as we devour the seed corn
and eat the breeding stock.

We foul our air and water,
we bare our swords and boast.
We are but dying parasites
upon a dying host.

Are we too obstinate to learn,
too scarce of wit to know
that the closing words in the Book of Life
will be "I told you so"?

The buck stops there

In reviewing my deeds of the past
that have brought me to sorrow or shame,
I can trace each event just far enough back
to arrive at somebody to blame.

Out of my hands

How amusing,
   how quaint,
      how droll,
to have to be,
  always,
       in control.

The planet spins,
the oceans roll;
look who thinks
she's in control.

Simple request

Use, at the end, no extraordinary means,
take no heroic measures.
Let his death be simple and serene,
the last of his life's uncomplicated pleasures.

Old gods

Precious and fragile are the old gods,
and due a gentle reverence.
We, who scorn the deification of ancestors,
have learned to despise weakness,
forgetting those who can yet bestow
humour for humour
and a poignant distillation
of humanity.
Give them respect and tenderness,
their worshippers grow strong
through singularity,
so many blessings for so few to share,
such wealth of memory,
such treasure of experience.
Give homage to the old gods,
they are the wise, courageous ones
who go before,
whose lives are sacrifice
to smoothe our path,
in whose cracked mirrors
we come to know our faces.

Personal opinion on an old philosophical question

The falling tree will make no sound
with no one there to hear it fall.
Indeed, without observing eyes,
there isn't any tree at all.

A lesson from Mum

My mother, God bless her,
is over eighty
and she hasn't got much time
for hypocrites.

    She's been around
    and she's heard it all
    and you can say
    almost anything
    in front of her,

        – as long as you mean it.

The First Noble Truth

Whom the gods would teach,
they frequently anoint
with suffering.
                      Okay!

I get the point.

Earth Day – 1990

A clean air bill,
comprehensive and extensive,
would be too expensive.
Laws too rigid? – No compliance.
The president and the industrial giants
have an alliance.
The public's right to respiration
dies a rasping, gasping death.
There'll be no resuscitation,
Bush will veto legislation.
You and I, in desperation,
can hold our breath.

The sophisticates

We nursed our illusion of love,
for its death was too tasteless to mention,
and cultured our mutual scorn
for suburban and civic convention.
We were two of the beautiful folk,
not the rabble that whistles and sniffs.
We were charming and witty and chic
and too civil for squabbles and tiffs.
We directed our barbs with aplomb
while carefully keeping our heads,
for if we had aimed at those we most loathed
we'd have torn one another to shreds.

Safe for the moment

I mark the passing of the whales,
the elephants, the redwood trees,
and thank the heavens we have found
no earthly use for chickadees.

Healing

The pain that sears the brain,
that burns through tissue, nerve and bone,
is just the body, learning
what the mind has known.

The mind that knows just negativity
and finds this life a sad and sorry place
can seal the spirit into suffering
and steal the body from its state of grace.

But love and joy forgive the shame
and cast out fear and lack
and liberate the soul and heart
and give the body back.

Purification

I keep my kuti spic and span
and tidy as I go.
I wash my bowl as best I can
and keep my profile low.
I try to keep defilements
from cluttering the place
and sometimes, when there's no one home,
the Buddha wears my face.

People

People
  we don't know
  are killing
people
  we don't know,
  neglecting
people
  we don't know
  and hurting
people
  we don't know
    and
  if we don't know
  how suffering feels
    to
people
  we don't know,
  we don't know
people.

Omigods

My gods dispense, in mystifying ration,
malevolence, capriciousness, compassion.
Beneath such doubtful benisons as theirs,
I beg indifference in all my prayers.

May

May above all and every,
May out of sheer delight,
from the emerald blush
to the promised lush
and the Buddha moon at night.

May for the dandelions,
reflections of the sun.
Of the twelve we're dealt,
I have always felt
May is the winning one.

In May the courting sparrows
are puffed with peacock pride,
and daffodils
adorn the hills
when May is far and wide.

May for the birds and flowers,
for fragrance fresh and pleasant,
for the gentle grace
of a pansy's face
and blessings ever present.

The world can sometimes overwhelm,
as day by day we cope
with disgust and despair
but, where May is, there
is always joy and hope.

I do knot

Marriage need not be oppressive, I guess.
I tend to be terrified, though,
that once you pronounce that indenturing yes
you forfeit the right to say no.

Things are sometimes what they seem

Mind on breath
as it pulls and pushes;
consciousness arises
to an object in the bushes.
A momentary glimpse,
a lightning-flash referral.
Here comes a squirrel's tail,
it must be a squirrel.
        And instant recognition
        just like that. –
        You don't get a squirrel's tail
        following a cat.

New Year's Resolution II

Before I suggest
that I know what is best,
I will stop and consider it twice.
It may spare me the sight
of the pitiful plight
of somebody who took my advice.

White Boots poem

I am wearing white boots.
It's the twenty-fourth of May
and sultans of the stylish say
it's allowed,
it's all right,
it's okay
to be shod in white
today.
So I am wearing white boots,
kicking up my heels
in a syncopated step which feels
like it's finally, fully
fairly and finely spring.
      Most of the time
      I slip and sneak
      and disguise myself
      in occult chic,
      but today it's a totally different thing
      in the light of the bright white right of spring.
It's been raining
for the last six days
and this morning
it looked so much like a flurry
that I was tempted to go back inside in a hurry
and put on something furry,
but I'm leaving all furs with their original owners
and putting on white boots,
because it's spring
and the white boot season waits for no one.
It's been spring for two months,
– which has taken me until today to remember
because it's colder now than it was in December.

Nevertheless, I am wearing white boots.
I think that's reasonable,
we don't get a long time that they're seasonable,
– for after Labour Day
the fashion gurus say
it's too late for white boots.
      Nine weeks after the vernal equinox
      I have taken off my long woolen socks
      and my fleece-lined knickers
      and everyone smiles and snickers
      as I skid on the sidewalks
      in springtime boots.
           They're not winter boots, you know,
           they're not made for ice and snow.
But whatever the weather,
there's spring in my stride
and a spring in my step
and I'm warm inside
and the coolest, hottest lady on the street,
tapping my toes in a white boot beat
with my thermostat set on springtime heat
and my springtime heart with the springtime yearning
to be there with both ends of my candle burning
the moment some young man's fancy starts turning.

Single minded
and
selfish to the end

Marry, they urge,
    or the future will find you
   a lonely and selfish
      old fusser and fretter.

I have been lonely
and I have been married.

      Lonely is better.

Limitations

     The universe is frightening
to those who think it so.
     There are so many things to see,
so many things to know,
so many explorations
and paths that come and go
that many folks are threatened
by the the ceaseless ebb and flow.
     The insecurity of choice
persuades their status quo
to build a fence around itself
to give them room to grow.

Mantra

Flow water and wind,
bear away concept and thought.
This is not mine, nor my soul.
This I am not.

All that is born and dies,
all that is fettered or free,
all that arises and passes,
this is not me.

I am not feeling or form,
memory, mind or emotion.
I am a cell in the body of God,
a wave which embraces the ocean.

Runaway

With crack in her bloodstream
and booze on her breath,
she stands on the corner,
soliciting death.
The streets and the pimps
and the johns are behind her.
Life has been merciless.
Death will be kinder.

As my father lay dying

As my father lay dying,
we brought him gifts,
    gadgets and electronic toys,
    squares and beads of coloured glass
        for his leaded pictures,
    all manner of things to coax him
        from the contemplation of oblivion.
With spicy foods and forbidden morsels
we sought to tempt his appetite,
    which savoured only cessation.
With laughter and love,
    plans and memories
we tried to lure him
    as he wandered from us
        toward a new companion.
We could not bribe him with life
or bully him with tears.
We could not hold him.

Death, having been long ignored,
avoided, eluded,
through ponderous persistence
triumphed at last
and had, at the end,
his undivided attention.

Weeded out

Having succeeded in my quest for anonymity,
slipping like a chameleon into invisibility,
escaping the worldly toils
of praise and blame,
notoriety and fame,
I stand alone and muted
at the edge of conversation,
   a colourless weed on the verge of a flower bed,
remarking silently
that I am become
too nondescript for cultivation.

Foretaste

    I tasted death today.
It took my breath away.
    Two tiny grains,
like desert sand
upon my tongue,
sucked from me
everything moist and young,
emptying each lung
to a dry, exsanguinated rasping.
    The living wind
rushed from my throat.
    In terror,
I retrieved it
with a desperate gasping
and blessed each resurrected breath
thinking, it takes so little,
oh so little death.

Lioness' share

I envisioned a division of our labours
so that all need never fall to only one,
but his single contribution to the housework
was to tell me how he liked to see it done.

Showtime

    I waken to a shimmering.
  The molecules of morning,
      freed by sleep
      from coalescing concepts,
shudder themselves
into daylight conformity
with my perceived reality.
    Before my eyelid curtains part,
the unbound dancers
resume their roles
according to my choreography
and dress the stage
for yet another scene
of life as I see it.

April

All the bare winter
the willows have wept
and, sombre,
a somnolent company kept
till golden they waken
and verdantly swing
in a fervent fandango
and,
     bango,
          it's spring.

No–body witness

Every pain I ever knew
has surfaced, and some others, too.
In fact, I haven't any doubt
my eyeballs just turned inside out.
With all this suffering, it's clear
I'm fortunate there's no me here.

Star dust

Spiral and spin and swirl
through shadows of space, and make
a shimmering twist in time
in your vortical wake.

Dust of the death of a star
seeding a star's gestation,
matter born of the Word,
bear my illumination.

From the no-beginning which was
to beyond each sun's last ember,
spin me back into light.
Light of my flesh, remember.

Jane makes hospital calls

She'll explain and explain,
again and again,
how I've brought on myself
every sorrow and pain;
so I try just to smile,
not to cry or complain,
lest I'm given the gospel
according to Jane.

Ten seconds to midnight

                                        – a round

What a downright shame,
what a damn disgrace
to be a member
of the human race.
What joy,   We've blood on our hands
what ecstacy,   and egg on our face
what bliss,   and we've made an unholy
to be a part   mess of the place.
of the whole
of this.
In the midst of the mess
to mightily know
we can plant a garden
and help it grow.

Reconciliation

　　I am not at home
in this body.
　　I have searched
down the ages
for a shape
that would suit me,
the senses
that would shape me
back
to undifferentiation.
　　Only as I lie upon the earth,
as spiders web me over
and ants cover me about
with reverential leaves,
do I send root tendrils
from my pores
to weld me, meld me
into oneness.
　　Down deep
beneath her skin
I join Earth's pulsing tides
in their slow rolls of ecstacy
and place myself,
unborn,
into the womb of Mother.

Laboratory rabbits

In quivering ranks of agony they crouch,
defending the beautiful people from itches and rashes,
a conscript army, fighting to the death
that we, who have blackened our souls, may darken our lashes.

The survivor

She does not cover her baldness.
Her open nakedness challenges
and defies.
Nonchalantly, she wears her scars
like livid battle ribbons.
Life is the prize.
Incredulous and aghast,
I stare,
then hurriedly avert my eyes,
humbled by simple courage,
ashamed of fear
that I cannot disguise
before this messenger
of death so painfully postponed,
this herald of my own demise.

No trouble at all

No need to flee from trouble,
just look it in the eye
and tell yourself
that you can see
its bright side, if you try,
and a cloud on your horizon
simply means that, by and by,
there's every chance
that there will be
a rainbow in your sky.

Design fault

Time is an asset
too fickle to trust.
I don't have forever
to do as I must.
I haven't got always
to do as I will.
I'm under the gun
and I'm over the hill.
My span is uncertain,
its ending ordained.
Don't ring down the curtain
until I've complained.
I'd get it together,
I'd master the art
but, faster and faster,
I'm falling apart
and answers elude me
as, little by little,
my brain grows more spongey,
my bones grow more brittle.
It's tougher to think
and it's rougher to do
as I sway on the brink
of making it through.
The longer the tooth,
the greater the hunger.
Why aren't we born old
and designed to grow younger?

Toronto – Victoria Day

Fairy lanterns float upward
from every corner open to the sky
and the great, glowing lance
thrusts, stupa-like,
into indigo night,
launching consciousness to heaven.

Strewn across the harbour,
gem-encrusted clusters
and jewelled strands
flicker with internal fires.

Far from my forests
and my sylvan dreams,
I wonder.
There is so much light
in the city.

Fowl fornication

Last night on television,
the renowned British psychiatrist,
R.D. Laing,
expressed his opinion
that no one should be put in prison
because they fucked a duck.
My thoughts went immediately
to the duck –
        mature?
        consenting?
        male or female?
and was there   protection from pregnancy and STD's?
          anal or vaginal penetration?
            enough foreplay to guarantee lubrication?
Was the duck provocatively dressed?
        sexually aggressive?
Did it say no but mean maybe?
Was it a platonic acquaintance?
    a blind date?
      or a complete stranger?
and was it driven home
or just dumped on a deserted road
to waddle bedraggledly back to the dorm?
Will this incident
leave it permanently scarred
or roll like water off its back?
Where are the animal rights activists?
Are we to have no policy statement from the SPCA?
Has the Humane Society abandoned its principals?

Let the shrinks busy themselves
with the duck fuckers,
be they neurotic, psychotic, maladjusted,
antisocial, sociopathic or merely presbyopic;
my concern is for
the mallards, the pintails,
the scoters, the mergansers,
the violated
Daisys, Daffys and Donalds
whose ruffled feathers
elicit no outcry
from the flock of complacent quacks.

Keeping on

Doing and doing,
I'm busy pursuing
the dream of a lifetime of ease.
Some day I'll be done
with what has to be done

and then I will do as I please.

New Year's Day – 1990

Old Man Time
has made his rounds.
Last year's calendar
lies among the orange rinds,
the bacon drippings
and the coffee grounds.
Last night's anesthetic
of old champagne
does not alleviate
this morning's fresh reshouldering
of ancient pain.

Too many toasts,
like bargains with the devil,
have brought a moment's respite
and a greater evil,
and happiness is not attained
by the decade or the year
but by the timeless instant
snatched, with thoughtless instinct,
between tomorrow's fear
and yesterday's despair.

I wish you fine
forgetful times
in which you do not care
that last year's journal of futility,
crumpled with the broken eggshells
  – this year's sins, next year's wages –
once hung in hopeful and serene sterility
where the new docket of your future days
presents in innocence and aspiration
its pristine pages.

Love thy neighbour

Jessica, my neighbour,
is too generous by far.
She feeds a flock of pigeons
who shit upon my car.
She feeds a horde of homeless cats
who love to fuck and fight
and howl outside my window
in the middle of the night.
Jessie's kindliness exceeds
a saintly superfluity.
I wish her a car of her very own
and auditory acuity.

Sic transit

Last night
in the subway station —
the monolithic wounded
stand
in a tableau of solitude,
like abandoned artifacts
of a forgotten civilization.
They carry no purses,
no briefcases,
no identities.
Their pockets are as empty
as their eyes.
They have not moved
in centuries.
Ten thousand years from now
they will be found,
petrified,
in the dust and rubble
of our indifferent transitoriness,
and alien scientists
will solemnly debate
their astronomical significance.

The pessimist

Life is a foe
that he pommels and trammels
with ultimate straws
on incapable camels.

Thank you not

Thank you for sparing the time
from your intellectual quest
to concern yourself
with my petty affairs.
I'm so gratified that
somebody like you
should busy themselves
with my humble pursuits.
Not everyone cares.
I'm sure that my business will benefit
from your involvement
and your incisive analysis.
You're unspeakably kind
to have offered a piece of your mind
with your brain in the grip of paralysis.

Who?

I am a question
which asks itself of love
and the answer shows
the emptiness
from which impermanence arises
and into which it flows.
Out of the aggregates,
void though they be,
something incarnates
and calls itself me.

Mother of the bride

Strangely bereft,
oddly relieved,
at times she wept,
at other moments, smiled.
She celebrated
even as she grieved –
the parent bereaved,
weaned from the child.

Cycling…

...bi, tri, and motor –
Life has its ups and downs
its go-around, come-around,
spin-around
in and out
changes.
    – Cycles, cycles, cycles
spiralling
to wherever they take us
and almost back,
but not quite,
because cycles aren't circles,
and every old familiar
sunrise and sunset
finds us some new place
in this
expanding universe's space.
        evolution, revolution, convolution, devolution
        becoming, turning, twisting, mutating
Tomorrow will discover us
different from today
for every borrowed breath
mixes us roundly, soundly,
inexplicably, inextricably
into the cosmos,
        adds and subtracts,
        takes what we never had,
        gives what we cannot own,
        as we dissolve
        and coalesce,
        bipedalling the velocities
        which speed us on
        our helical hegiras
        into transformation.

Unhappy hour

From cocktail party conversation,
save me, oh sweet charity,
from empty clatter-chatter
and in-earnest insincerity,
competitive name dropping
and comparative achievement
and the endless rote of marriage, birth,
betrothal and bereavement.
Spare me the flippancy of fools,
the saws of learned folk
and the thirteenth repetition
of an unamusing joke.
Deliver me from cackling, clucking,
yapping, bleating, braying
and the sickening embarrassment
of hearing what I'm saying.

Sound mind – unsound body.

When I'm struck by the onset of illness,
I just don't know how to behave –
shall I let people think I'm enlightenedly well
or sick, but incredibly brave?

Short leash

I'll never sail through infinite space,
exploring the galaxies ancient and new,
or sift through the universe lying within
as the mind, unconfined, is able to do.
I will not plumb the depths of the seas
or conquer the mountains, or master a few
of the myriad truths which are free to the free
if I'm fixed and attached to my own point of view.

Reality therapy

Concepts dissolve in a clear and cloudless sky,
the ocean washes my conversations away,
the striving sleeps, the restless cravings die
   and blue
      is the only truth I know today.

Overextended

I don't bounce back like I used to.
I've given it lots of thought.
I've been in so much hot water
I think my elastic's shot.

Post-mortem

He died of chaos,
a surfeit of randomness,
a butterfly function
disordering
the equations of his heart,
foretelling metamorphosis.

Elaboration

    Yesterday is a half-forgotten dream,
a prank played by recollection,
quarter-turning the signpost
at some crossroad
of the neural pathway
leading to historical fiction.
    I do not know a past
that has not been embroidered
by the tricky picky sticky fingers of time.
    Your memory
      is a tale I tell myself
time
   upon
     flowered
     coloured
     satin-stitched
     French-knotted
     decorated
time,
–   a subjective truth
    having little to do
    with unadorned veracity.

Deux ex tenuated

Don't tell me about some omnipotent God,
– that all must befall as He planned;
I'd rather believe He intended no harm
but some things just got out of hand.

City mouse

With mental claw and moral tooth,
I fight the subtle threat of youth
past Yonge Street's neon bars
on summer evenings, and recall
Superior's lonely shore and all
companionable stars,
the soothing voice of water and
the ancient rocks, the healing land.

In concrete heights, I brood
on silent, undiluted night
where moon and stars were ample light
for gentle solitude.

Why am I hidden from the sky?
Why does the city make me shy?
What road enticed me here
where memory weighs the price it pays
in menacing dark and frantic days,
and finds it is too dear?

Starlings

An undulating cloud,
a whirling globe
progresses through space,
    unwinding in spirals,
    aligning into ranks
        which pass back upon each other
        like soldiers on parade
        or square dancers
            moving from do-si-do's
            to right-and-left-through's
            into grand chains
            of the complexity
            with which the Sufis weave
            their tapestries of fluid devotion.

Now they swoop, turn
separate and merge,
    atoms in motion,
    creating complex molecules
    with alchemical additions
            subtractions,
            transformations.

Like obsidian light,
they flow
in waves and particles,
    a multi-celled organism
    telepathically choreographing
    a spontaneous dance
        where wings attend
        the metronome
        of collective mind-beats,
            seventeen per second.

New ground

One needs to clear the underbrush
to find the room to grow.
What keeps me most from learning
is thinking that I know.

Hope springs

    My Aunt B,
who is a retired English teacher,
       – having been,
         I hasten to postulate,
         an exceptionally good one,
tells me that poetry
is no longer being taught as it was
in the high schools.
    I rejoice,
with the relief
of a loser breaking even.
    Perhaps,
even now,
there impends
an unconditioned generation
who will not inform me,
upon first meeting,
that they do not care for poetry.

Youth, passing

        You are too young to wear the scent of roses.
        Roses are for the autumn afternoons
of staid and stately dowagers,
arrayed in dignity and attar
as the trees are shrouding themselves
in gold and scarlet
and the gardens turn their sere September faces
toward winter.
        My grandmama wore roses
and smelled of crisp, dead petals
and decomposing memories.
There will be time enough
for the long perfume of roses.
        If the aroma of your own sweet self
does not content you,
save roses for your season of decline
and take a springtime fragrance.
Wear lilly of the valley
and smell like April passing
too swiftly for the odour of decay.

Croaked

I had a little froggie and he got squashed flat,
he was hiding under the welcome mat.
I warned him a dozen times about that
but frogs don't listen.
                I'm getting a cat.

Farewell

Where the waves are bluer than a mermaid's eyes,
we cast him to the winds
and the ocean currents.
        Now he is everywhere.
There shall be none
who may not breathe him on the air
or taste his essence in all things,
and now the love we bore him
is owed to all,
        for he is everyone.
                His wake is the gulf stream waters
                as he wakens to the infinite.

Always the longing

Always the longing
sleeping in my heart
like a bird in the nest,
like a fox in the lair.
No game, sensation, concept
can build a wall to keep it out —
long since, its domicile
has been established there.
Leaping to flame,
awakening to incandescent heat
from a somnolent, ever-present ember,
it burns my breath away
and all that I can say
is "Yes, Lord, I remember."

Busy, busy

Searching for freedom,
filled with desire,
ever creating the me;
seeking, selecting,
rejecting, collecting,
too busy looking to see.

Reminiscences

Moist shadows of fresh dreams
burn dimly at the hearth,
old dessicated memories
burn bright.
Let us not speak tonight of love
old friend;
let us not speak of love tonight.
Tender new dreams
are still too green a fuel
for bygone passions'
sacrificial pyre;
when they are dried and brittle,
we shall warm
our cold, old hopes and hearts
around their fire.

Prolonged adolescence

Senility attends
the fate which shapes our ends.
Oh Heavens, let me not abandon hope with it.
Let childishness assuage
the terror of old age
till I become adult enough to cope with it.

A loner with a lover

A loner with a lover
has a tricky situation
which potentially is weighty and repressive.
He must use all of his talents
to keep solitude in balance
with togetherness, so neither gets excessive.

A loner with a lover
must indulge in conversation
when the ecstacy of silence begs attention.
The frivolity of chatter
about subjects that don't matter
is a topic which he should neglect to mention.

A loner with a lover
must forego the still elation
of the clear, transparent moment, rarely known
in the kindly meant distraction
of unending interaction
where a loner cannot call his mind his own.

Claustrophobic incidents
require a long recuperation
or he tends to fits of jittery moroseness,
and a loner with a lover
needs a fortnight to recover
from a weekend of unmitigated closeness.

A loner sometimes celebrates
the absence of sensation
and the freedom from a well-beloved touch.
A loner with a lover
may resent the constant hover
and solicitude which ministers too much.

A loner with a lover
may encounter irritation
when his train of thought is frequently derailed
by attention too effusive
as he courts the Muse elusive
who prefers, in crowds, to keep her features veiled.

The lover of a loner
may express the inclination
to pack her bags and pack it in for good
    for she often feels neglected,
      even totally rejected,
and the loner is inclined to wish she would.

A loner and his lover
need a touch of inspiration
to arrive at a relationship providing
shared and solitary pleasure
to them both in equal measure
and enough of it to keep them from deciding
that the whole thing doesn't merit the frustration
and the ardor isn't worth the aggravation.

In my prime

Age has it compensations.
I'm here to tell the tale
that, as my mirror lost its charm,
my eyes began to fail.

    Memory loss is not so bad,
    it makes some room for inspiration.
    Lobes too tightly packed can cause
    mnemonic constipation.

   You don't get nothin' for nothin',
   my haggard reflection howls.
   The hollows that give me cheekbones
   are purchased with teeth, by jowls.

Growing older has its perks;
I've done my time,
I've done my duty.
And now it takes a perspicacious man
to see my beauty.

The intuitive rose

Only the rose can open up the rose
and never by coercion or command.
Instructed by the elements, it grows
and needs no intellect to understand.
Nourished by earth, encouraged by the sun,
it takes the rains and breezes for its own,
weaving all nature's wonders into one,
and rises to its destiny alone.
As it begins, it ends, untaught by man.
Within its heart, each generation knows
its purpose, its unfoldment and its plan,
transmitted by the archetypal rose.
    And all the wisdom it will ever need
    lies in the intuition of the seed.

Seas apart

I thought that somehow you might soothe me,
now I'm in a terrible fix,
I'm troubled much more than before you appeared.
It's clear that we never will mix.

You're just too much oil for my water.
With compromise out of my reach
and, finding that I cannot swallow you whole,
I must wash you back up on the beach.

Forgive me my lack of acceptance,
the choice I've no choice but to make.
I'm vast and I'm deep but there's only so much
that even the ocean can take.

Another love poem – for my old friends

Lovingly, I leave them
and I do not doubt they love me
but the waters of forgetfulness
close silently above me
as I sink from their remembrance,
though my absence may be fleeting.
So we have to fall in love again
with every meeting.

Rapunzel in the city

       Moonlight,
brighter than neon
and fluorescence,
silvers my kitchen floor
around the shadows
of jade plant
and lemon geranium.
       Stronger
in its magic
than glass and steel and concrete,
it plucks me from my tower,
plunging me
out of fairy tales
into freedom
where
the moon and I,
having seen eye to eye
on reality,
admit no princes.

A gift of ammonite ...

... an agate slice of the Jurassic
   from our reptile past
   which saw the birth of mammals
         first flowers of plants
         rising of conifers,
spiralling life form
   fossilized and petrified
   polished to adamantine brilliance,
betokening
   in this Quaternary present
the path which
   through the eons
consciousness has travelled,
   must travel,
      inward and outward
to its open ended
    self centred
       emptiness,
            its crystal destiny ...

I wish

I wish
      that love were not my last resort.
I wish
      compassion rose before disgust.
I wish
      I did not have to learn
        this painful way
          but if I must
            I must.

Seasoning

It's April
and I am comforted
    with juvenescence,
    with branches appliqued to sky
        in lacy imminence
and buds that cannot contain
their excitement,
    with last year's robins
        on about this year's business.
Everywhere pulses
    with traditional renewal,
    continuity of innovation.
Caught for a moment
in the impersonality
of becoming,
I am no longer
spectator,
    neither devotee
    nor critic,
but simply,
    supremely,
    sublimely,
    seminally,
spring.

Passing through

I learned what yes meant.
I learned what no meant.
I learned love
in and of the moment,
to let it go
and let it be.
    Whatever returns from extinction
    will not be me.

Wake-up call

It was tranquillity
that rocked me,
    carried me high,
    buried me deep.
But it was suffering
that shocked me
    from my sleep.

Taxidermy (stuff this)

Most things I handle coolly
but some things make me burn,
like the tax I'm taxed on stamps I buy
to mail my tax return.

The great, collective shame

came again this morning
and I wept
for starvation
and vivisection,
for war
and ignorance
and greed,
– for my self-centred guilt.
      And I wept
for the pain of autumn
and eternal winter
on a ravaged, desert sphere,
for meaning mocked
and for doomed existence.
      Then begging absolution,
I remembered the compassion,
the simple humility
of the great ones,
    the calm and wholesome currents,
    in a corrosive, seething, sea
and I recalled that even saints
have had their clouded vision,
    their astigmatisms;
yet,
they have ceased to do evil,
they have learned to do good.
      So I may find forgiveness
for my repentant impotence.
Still, I would wish,
in expiation and in restitution
and, perhaps, in arrogance,
that I, alone,
might die for my sins.

For Ruth

Though Mara entices,
solicits, proposes,
I know I am sitting.
I know where my nose is.

Observation by an almost complete donkey

With impossible carrots
on endless sticks,
I keep myself doing
my half-assed tricks.

Epitaph

Don't grave my stone
with virtues that
I never had
and haven't got.
Just mention,
if there's space to fill,
I spoke no ill
and laughed a lot.

Nothing doing

Nothing for clinging,
nothing for holding,
only emptiness
opening,
unfolding.

No beginning,
no ending,
only nothing,
changing,
blending.

Nowhere to go,
nothing to do,
nothing but nothing
passing through,
leaving nothing
under the sun,
only the all,
only the one.

Nothing to be,
nothing to say,
only arising
passing away.

Extinction

... Elephants for their tusks,
bears for their gall bladders,
rhinoceroses for their horns,
leopards for their skins,
whales for their oil,
buffalo for their flesh,
egrets for their plumes ...
    I thought, perhaps,
    that the sabre-toothed tiger
    might have considered
    primitive man
    a delicacy,
    but it must have been
    the other way round.

November sixteenth

Last night
I dreamed of my father
and awoke knowing
that somewhere,
in some well-merited, auspicious birth,
an earth dragon scorpion child,
having conquered death,
is preparing to grapple with life
and wrestle the world
to its adoring knees.

Highest authority

I went to Massey Hall, to hear
the Dalai Lama speak.
He said that he is growing old;
it made my knees go weak.
It made my hand begin to shake,
it made my blood run colder.
His Holiness is getting old
and I am three years older.

Global concern

A semicircle
rotating on its diameter
brings about a sphere.

If I turn
and turn again,
turn around,
come around,
come about,
go around,
return ...
will I accomplish
another dimension?

Silk purse

Let the event of my death
evoke more celebration than mourning
and, given my life may have failed to inspire,
let it stand, in the end, as a warning.
My virtues are seldom and scant;
my errors and sins have been ample.
Whatever the cost, it will not have been lost
if I serve as a horrid example.

Discretion

Why bruise the sensibilities of those
whose vision does not correspond with ours?
There is no need to speak of Buddha fields
to those who do not see or smell the flowers.

In my dreams

In my dreams
I am younger, slimmer, sexier,
all those things that the TV commercials
say I ought to want to be,
and swains and beaus and suitors
of the most discerning kind –
the ones who love you for your mind –
cast themselves at the freshly pedicured feet
of the white-robed, well-groomed, sweet,
younger, slimmer, sexier me.

And I awaken pondering the thought
that I somehow unconsciously have bought
the picture that the image makers sell
and I hurry to the mirror,
less affronted than amused,
to affirm that ever dearer
is the image dreams refused
in my fast asleep rejection,
  and my own devotion tell
  to the older, fatter, more androgynous reflection
  that serves my daylight purposes
  so well.

… But then again,
a lifting of the jowls,
a liposuction of the hips,
a dyeing of the grey
might keep the old inevitable at bay
till I have grown mature enough to cope
with the abandoning of hope
that lies in the denial of dream,
and I have grown facile enough at selling myself
the half truths and total fictions
which I seem to be
endlessly telling myself.

Intermittent affair

We met and we parted and met once again;
we pooled our great passions and flung our small fling.
Like the romance of the moth and the firefly,
ours was an on-again, off-again thing.

Minor move

Merely a low-key shift,
　　less a leap than a drift,
　　　　nothing bold or dramatic,
　　　　　　leaving only an echo, and just
　　　　　a few specks of dust
　　　　　　in an empty attic.

Capital litter

Successful politicians,
I have long suspected,
rise far above the common man
the moment they're elected
and justify their high estate,
their rarified existence,
by sinning somewhat subtler sins
and sinning at a distance.

Shame on me

I have been swindled and duped and bilked,
I have been gulled and conned.
I've had my human kindness milked,
my patience gone beyond.
I've been bamboozled and beguiled
by trumpery and trickery.
Fortune, for some, may well have smiled,
for me she has just been snickery.
I may deserve the skeptic's scorn
for a nature too naive
but that's how I've been since I was born,
so eager to believe,
so slow and reluctant to read the truth
inscribed by the cynic's pen.
So tell me love's little lies, sweet youth,
I can be fooled again.

Disorient express

Outside my window, the sound of a train
carries me gone to my castle in Spain,
travels me right off the track.
Give me a moment, I'll get back.

... to the world

Because there has never been
more occasion for sorrow,
more opportunity for despair,
more reason for regret,
I choose joy,
unreasoning, unreasoned joy,
unmoved by hope and fear
by what has gone and what will come,
by cloud and shadow and impending apocalypse.

I have seen the bottomless abyss
that can be floored
only by madness
or by faith.
And I have known the anxious, doubting mind
to move from fear
through affirmation.
And having learned
the secret of generosity,
I make the gift,
even to myself,
of joy.

And to you and to all,
that spark which leaps,
fusing heart to heart,
that choiceless choice
born by struggle out of surrender,
that joy which is
the mother, daughter, twin
of love.

Travel fare

At the smorgasbord
of the mind,
I choose to feed the heart
only on breath.

The mind doesn't mind,
having just left
on the last train of thought
for tomorrow.

Requiem

I cannot stray to faraway
for memories pursue,
the little habits of my heart,
the little ramblings of my thought,
the little patterns of my life
all bring me back to you.
The pain will dull to now and then
when loss is not so new,
still every old remember when
will lead me home to you.
And never is a sentence
which no shackled soul can do,
so I'll recall with joy that I'm
within the universal mind
that comforts me and sets me free
and binds me up in you.
My sunset songs and moonlight dreams,
my mossy trails and silver streams,
my every is and all my seems
are in and out
and all about
the everywhere of you.

Imperfect love

Sometimes the fear
it scares me so
my heart beats
like to bust.
When will I
  when will I
  when will I learn
to trust?

Cosmos

eternal blossom
whose petals of creation
unfold emptiness,
manifestation
out of void
return to void
heart of the matter

Broken silence

At his bedside
in the still void,
the endless, eternal emptiness,
I stood,
taking stock of pain
as pacemaker and monitor,
in electronic conversation,
spoke obscene mockery
of a shattered heart.

The sycophants

They fawn and they flatter,
they sit at his feet
while praising his talent and fame
and that is the service
which all of them pay
for the pleasure of dropping his name.

Better late

My salad days are wilted and past.
How did I get so old so fast?
My lettuce is tossed, my greens are flung;
I'll have to hurry if I want to die young.

Immediate family

Not by the blood
or by the gene pool linked,
but by the instant recognition
of spirit meshed with spirit;
love knowing love,
to all love relative.
Not through a chance of birth
but through a choice of kinship,
we join ourselves
in multidimensional unity,
seeds of the same flowering,
flowers of the same seeding.
        This is my family.

Awedball

Everywhere I come
I find myself.
Wherever I go
I leave myself.
I am in all things
and everything dissolves in me.
I am both sides of the question,
the top and bottom too,
and all the ins and outs,
yea, even unto the nth dimension.
I am acquainted
with all life
and death will take me nowhere
I have not been before.
But this familiarity
breeds contempt
only for contempt.
Knowing
begets and fosters
worship and wonder.

Poet emeritus

       He sits across the coffee cups,
grey and sometimes absent,
an ancient eunuch,
bland and civil,
dispensing sugar, cream
and bowdlerized reminiscences.
       But I am not deceived.
I know, behind his smile,
he visits lusty realms,
unexpurgated memories
which spark the pale coolness
of his modest eyes.
       We do not speak of passion.
His public declarations
are not mentioned
in our private audience.
But I have not the slightest doubt
he knows
that I have read his pagan poetry.

Pollution control

Mother's looking sickly.
Mother's feeling lowly.
Mother's dying quickly.
Let's poison her more slowly.

Disciple

I endeavor to teach
what I have yet to reach.
You may think me bemused and benighted,
but although I am blind
leading the blind,
I am leading the blind to the sighted.

Koan in circles

"What is memory?" I ask,
   remembering
      that I have asked before.

Another lesson from Mum

My mother remarked today
that she is getting
a little forgetful.

I maintain
that she has long been forgetful,
she has just now noticed it.

I call that mindful.

But, then again,
she always has been.

Out of play

Yesterday,
    for the first time
        in a long time,
I was propositioned,
    by a seventy-year-old
    hurdy gurdy player
        on Bloor Street
    who said he liked the way I walked.

I walked on.

Concrastination

I offer a word of advice for those troublesome times
when abhorrences harry you –
      make it a habit to shovel today's shit today
      or tomorrow's will bury you.

Still gestating

I don't know what's the matter,
I am sober and I'm stable
and I live within my precepts
just as well as I am able.
I'm not ruled by greed or hatred
and I rarely break a vow
and if Jesus really loved me
I'd have seen the light by now.

Moment um

Nouns in flux,
verbs in motion,
words in pursuit
of fleeing meaning,
concepts seeking definition
in symbols,
    reality reaches
    for reassuring metaphor
    to bind
    the illusion of completion,
        but no-thing
        flows
        through the interstices
        of explanation
            and Now
            thunders down
            the fences of Eternity.

Rat race

No space, no time, no solitude;
crush and rush and panic rising –
      I'd be moved to eat my young
      – if they were less unappetizing.

Dealer's choice

I've tried to discover the meaning of life,
to learn what is valid and true
and many have said to me, "Do as I say"
and some have said, "Do as I do."
I've listened and struggled through joy and belief
and through disillusion and doubt
and life, to the best of my knowledge right now,
is about what I make it about.

Not even edgewise

        On the shadowed patio
where lovely people come and go,
candles flicker,
moisture glistens
on champagne flutes
and no one listens
        No one listens to the fiction
told in flawed or perfect diction,
stuttered, muttered,
calm or frantic,
or with accent mid-Atlantic,
some or none or all of those.
        No one listens to the prose
spoken shrilly by the silly
someones, in the hope absurd
there will hang on every word,
with attentiveness intense,
mute, admiring audience.
        Still, no little whit deterred,
speakers hoping to be heard
spin their yarns and tell their stories
through the torrid territories
to the hordes of heathen, grown
determined to relate their own.
        Round the potted palms they peer,
bent on borrowing an ear
for their sagas and narrations,
parables or recitations.
        But, though it speak of revelation,
newborn truth and inspiration,
none among the horrid herd
have a moment for a word
that communicates or christens
comprehension.
        No one listens.

Diligence

Life teaches me lessons,
   this one has been rough,
     you can have what you want
       only want it enough
and hearing the call
I fervently fall
to the one-pointed effort
of wanting it all.

Directions

Parental admonitions
resound within my head
as gently I am guided
and firmly I am led
by old internal echoes,
some thundering, some mild.
My father's voice says, "Act your age."
My mother's says, "My child."

Publix spectacle
or
Fraternizing with the anomie

The old transvestite
   in the yellow wig
     and I
        eyed each other
           in the checkout line
              at the supermarket.
Only one of us,
I reflected,
was having
an identity problem.

Relocation

Death is   eating away
                scratching away
                picking away
                tearing away   my fortress.
Those lives which were my sanctuary
are falling to
the relentless pressure,
the ravenous onslaught
of mortality,
    leaving me exposed,
    confused and unprotected,
    homeless among the ruins,
    or my demolished citadel.
By death,
being a fair landlord,
        who does not discriminate
        for race or age or creed or gender,
will not exclude fools
or the most bewildered of poets
and shall,
in timely restitution.
give me refuge.

The builder

With names as a hammer
and concepts as spikes,
in fear and confusion she slaves
to fashion security
out of the flux,
nailing the wind
to the waves.

Sometime

I cannot embrace him completely.
    Sometimes
the pain of proximity
is more than I can dare,
for he has betrayed me
with mortality
and I have retreated
to stand
at the dim edges of forgetfulness
and probe cautiously,
tentatively
at his memory,
ready to leap into distraction
should recollection
stray to tainted thought
of loss, abandonment, despair.
    Sometime
I shall touch him joyfully,
fearlessly, totally,
when I have forgiven him his death
and me my expectation
that he would live forever.

Gesture

We are past hope,
beyond regret;
the future is a joke.
But here,
on the volcano's slope,
I plant an oak.

Insight

Today I received a lesson
I couldn't have done without,
when something whispered in my ear
"It all works out."

And yes, I thought, it all works out
I must trust that's the way it goes
for worry and fear obscure the view
of how totality flows.

It all works out and it all comes round
and it's all some kind of test
where all you can do is the best you can do
and grace will do the rest.

For previous titles and poetry readings please contact the publisher.

By Linda Stitt

REFLECTIONS FROM A DUSTY MIRROR
WHAT DO YOU FEED A UNICORN?
YESTERDAY'S POETRY
IT WAS TRUE AT THE TIME